muffins
& quick breads

muffins
& quick breads

SIMPLE RECIPE IDEAS FOR DELICIOUS
TRADITIONAL HOME BAKING

LINDA FRASER

LORENZ BOOKS

This edition first published by Lorenz Books
27 West 20th Street, New York, NY 10011

LORENZ BOOKS are available for bulk purchase for sales promotion
and for premium use. For details, write or call the sales director,
Lorenz Books, 27 West 20th Street, New York, NY 10011;
(800) 354-9657

Lorenz Books is an imprint of Anness Publishing Inc.

ISBN 0-7548-0268-X

Publisher: Joanna Lorenz
Senior Cookery Editor: Linda Fraser
Designer: Sheila Volpe
Photographers: Steve Baxter, Karl Adamson, Amanda Heywood,
James Duncan and Michelle Garrett
Food for Photography: Wendy Lee, Jane Stevenson and Elizabeth Wolf-Cohen
Props Stylists: Blake Minton and Kirsty Rawlings

Front Cover: William Lingwood, Photographer; Helen Trent, Stylist;
Sunil Vijayakar, Home Economist

Previously published as part of the *Creative Cooking Library* series

Printed in Hong Kong/China

1 3 5 7 9 10 8 6 4 2

CONTENTS

BAKING TECHNIQUES

Baking your own muffins and breads is easy and satisfying, even if you're a beginner. Just follow the recipes and the tips, hints, and step-by-step techniques and you'll get perfect results every time.

1 ▲ For liquids measured in cups: Use a glass or clear plastic measuring cup. Put the cup on a flat surface and pour in the liquid. Bend down and check that the liquid is exactly level with the marking on the cup, as specified in the recipe.

Equipment
To be able to cook efficiently and with pleasure, you need good equipment. That is not to say that you should invest in an extensive collection, but a basic range of cookware is essential. Buy the best equipment you can afford, adding more as your budget allows. Well made equipment lasts and is a sound investment; inexpensive cookware is likely to dent, break, or develop "hot spots" where food will stick and burn, so will need replacing. Flimsy tools will make food preparation more time consuming.

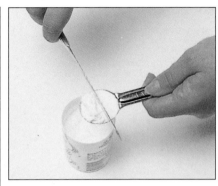

2 ▲ For measuring dry ingredients in a cup or spoon: Fill the cup or spoon. Level the surface even with the rim of the cup or spoon, using the straight edge of a knife.

3 ▲ For liquids measured in spoons: Pour the liquid into the measuring spoon, to the brim, and then pour it into the mixing bowl.

4 ▲ For measuring flour in a cup or spoon: Scoop the flour from the canister in the measuring cup or spoon. Hold it over the canister and level the surface.

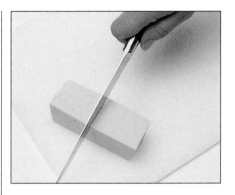

5 ▲ For measuring butter: With a sharp knife, cut off the specified amount following the markings on the wrapper.

6 ▲ For rectangular and square cake pans: Fold the paper and crease it with your fingernail to fit snugly into the corners of the pan. Then press the bottom paper lining into place.

7 ▲ To line muffin cups: Use paper cupcake liners of the required size. Or grease and flour the cups.

MAKING MUFFINS AND QUICK BREADS

As their name denotes, these bakes are fast and easy to make. The leavening agent reacts quickly with moisture and heat to make the muffins and breads rise, without the need for a rising period before baking.

The leavening agent is usually baking soda or baking powder, which is a mixture of baking soda and an acid salt such as cream of tartar. It will start to work as soon as it comes into contact with liquid, so don't mix the dry and liquid ingredients until just before you are ready to fill the muffin cups and bake.

In addition to the thick-batter quick breads discussed here, there are also quick breads such as biscuits that are made from soft doughs.

Granola Muffins
Make the batter from 1 cup flour, 2½ teaspoons baking powder, 2 tablespoons sugar, 1 cup milk, ¼ cup melted butter or corn oil, and 1 egg, adding 1¾ cups granola-type cereal with raisins to the dry ingredients. Pour into muffins cups (2½- to 2¾-inch diameter, 1½-inches deep). Bake in a preheated 400°F oven until golden brown, about 20 minutes. *Makes 10.*

1 ▲ For muffins: Combine the dry ingredients in a bowl. It is a good idea to sift the flour with the leavening agent, salt, and any spices to mix them. Add the liquid ingredients and stir just until the dry ingredients are moistened; the batter will not be smooth. Do not overmix in an attempt to remove all the lumps. If you do, the muffins will not be tender and will have tunnels in them.

2 ▲ Divide the batter evenly among the greased muffin cups (or line the cups with paper cupcake liners), filling them about two-thirds full. Bake until golden brown and a wooden skewer inserted in the center comes out clean. To prevent soggy bottoms, remove the muffins immediately from the cups to a wire rack. Let cool, and serve warm or at room temperature.

3 ▲ For fruit and/or nut breads: Method 1: Stir together all the liquid ingredients. Add the dry ingredients and beat just until smoothly blended. Method 2: Beat the butter with the sugar until the mixture is light and fluffy. Beat in the eggs followed by the other liquid ingredients. Stir in the dry ingredients. Pour the batter into a prepared pan (typically a loaf pan). Bake until a wooden skewer inserted in the center comes out clean. If the bread is browning too quickly, cover the top with foil.

4 ▲ Cool in the pan 5 minutes, then unmold onto a wire rack to cool completely. A lengthwise crack on the surface is characteristic of quick breads. For easier slicing, wrap the bread in wax paper and overwrap in foil, then store overnight at room temperature.

MAKING FOCACCIA AND BREAD STICKS

Italian flatbreads, such as focaccia, and bread sticks can be topped with herbs and seeds for tasty accompaniments or starters. Personalize them with combinations of your favorite ingredients for unusual snacks or split and fill flatbreads with ham or cheese for an Italian-style sandwich.

This basic dough can be used for other recipes, such as pizza. The dough may be frozen before it is baked, and thawed before filling.

1 ▲ For focaccia: Warm a mixing bowl by swirling some hot water in it. Drain. Place the yeast in the bowl, and pour on the warm water. Stir in the sugar, mix with a fork, and allow to stand until the yeast has dissolved and starts to foam, 5–10 minutes.

Working with Yeast
● A ¼-ounce package of active dry yeast contains 1 tablespoon. One cake of compressed fresh yeast is equivalent to a package of dry yeast. For quick-rising dry yeast, combine it with the flour and other dry ingredients, then add the liquids (which should be warmer than for ordinary active dry yeast). Or, follow recipe directions.
● If you are in any doubt about the freshness of the yeast, it is a good idea to "proof" it: set the yeast mixture in a warm place. After 5–10 minutes, the mixture should be foamy.

2 ▲ Use a wooden spoon to mix in the salt and about one-third of the flour. Mix in another third of the flour, stirring with the spoon until the dough forms a mass and begins to pull away from the sides of the bowl.

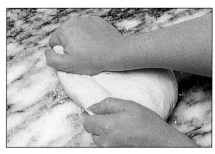

3 ▲ Sprinkle some of the remaining flour onto a smooth work surface. Remove the dough from the bowl and begin to knead it, working in the remaining flour a little at a time. Knead for 8–10 minutes. By the end the dough should be elastic and smooth. Form it into a ball.

4 Lightly oil a mixing bowl. Place the dough in the bowl. Stretch a damp dish towel or plastic wrap across the top of the bowl, and leave it to stand in a warm place until the dough has doubled in volume, about 40–50 minutes or more, depending on the type of yeast used. To test whether the dough has risen enough, poke two fingers into the dough. If the indentations remain, the dough is ready.

5 ▲ Punch the dough down with your fist to release the air. Knead for 1–2 minutes.

6 ▲ Brush a pan with oil. Press the dough into the pan with your fingers to a layer 1-inch thick. Cover and leave to rise for 30 minutes. Preheat the oven. Make indentations all over the focaccia with your fingers. Brush with oil, add filling and bake until pale golden.

7 ▲ For bread sticks: There's no need for the first rising. Divide dough into large walnut-size pieces and roll out on a floured surface with your hands, into thin sausage shapes. Transfer to a greased cookie sheet, cover and leave in a warm place for 10–15 minutes. Bake until crisp.

MAKING BISCUITS AND POPOVERS

Biscuits are quick breads made with a soft dough, based on flour and milk with a raising agent added. The dough may be rolled out and cut into shapes, or it may be dropped from a spoon onto a baking sheet, or molded.

Popovers are individual batter puddings, made in a similar way to Yorkshire puddings then flavored.

1 For biscuits: Sift together the dry ingredients into a large mixing bowl (flour, baking powder with or without baking soda). Add salt, cheese or herbs if making savory biscuits, or sugar and ground spices for sweet biscuits.

2 ▲ Add the fat (butter, margarine, shortening, etc.). With a pastry blender or two knives, cut the fat into the dry ingredients until the mixture resembles fine crumbs, or rub in the fat with your fingertips.

3 ▲ For rolled-out biscuits: Add the liquid ingredients (milk, cream, buttermilk, eggs). Stir with a fork until the dry ingredients are thoroughly moistened and will come together in a ball of fairly soft dough in the center of the bowl.

4 ▲ Turn the dough onto a lightly floured surface. Knead it very lightly, folding and pressing, to mix evenly, about 30 seconds. Roll or pat out the dough to ½- to ¾-inch thickness.

5 ▲ With a floured, sharp-edged cutter, cut out rounds or other shapes. Arrange on an ungreased baking sheet. Brush with beaten egg or cream. Bake until golden brown. Serve immediately.

6 ▲ For griddle biscuits: If using a well-seasoned cast iron griddle, there is no need to grease it. Heat it slowly and evenly. Put biscuit triangles or rounds on the hot griddle and cook for 4–5 minutes on each side or until golden brown and cooked through.

1 For popovers: Sift the flour into a large bowl along with other dry ingredients such as salt and ground black pepper. Make a well in the center of dry ingredients and put in the eggs, egg yolks and some of the liquid.

2 With a wooden spoon, beat together the eggs and liquid in the well just to mix them. Gradually draw in some of the flour from the sides, stirring vigorously.

3 When the mixture is smooth, stir in the remaining liquid. Stir just until the ingredients are combined – the trick is not to overmix.

4 ▲ Pour the batter into greased muffin cups or a muffin pan and bake until golden brown. Do not open the oven door during baking time or the popovers may fall. Run a knife around the edge of each popover to loosen, then turn out and serve hot.

Cutting Tips for Biscuits
- Be sure the cutter or knife is sharp so that the edges of the biscuit shapes are not compressed; this would prevent rising.
- Cut the shapes close together so that you won't have to reroll the dough more than once.
- If necessary, a short, sturdy drinking glass can be pressed into service as a cutter. Flour the rim well and do not press too hard.
- While cutting out, don't twist the cutter.

Sweet Muffins

Golden, moist muffins fresh from the oven are a
wonderful way to start the day and Cherry Marmalade
Muffins make an unusual breakfast treat. Enjoy them at
teatime, too, or whenever you feel like a delicious snack.
The recipes here are flavored with a tempting variety
of fresh and dried fruits, nuts and chocolate.

Prune Muffins

MAKES 12

1 egg

1 cup milk

¼ cup vegetable oil

¼ cup granulated sugar

2 tablespoons dark brown sugar

2 cups flour

2 teaspoons baking powder

½ teaspoon salt

¼ teaspoon grated nutmeg

¾ cup cooked pitted prunes, chopped

1 Preheat the oven to 400°F. Grease a 12-cup muffin tin or use paper liners.

2 Break the egg into a mixing bowl and beat with a fork. Beat in the milk and oil.

3 ▼ Stir in the sugars. Set aside.

4 Sift the flour, baking powder, salt, and nutmeg into a mixing bowl. Make a well in the center, pour in the egg mixture and stir until moistened. Do not overmix; the batter should be slightly lumpy.

5 ▲ Fold in the prunes.

6 Fill the prepared cups two-thirds full. Bake until golden brown, about 20 minutes. Let stand 10 minutes before unmolding. Serve warm or at room temperature.

Yogurt Honey Muffins

MAKES 12

4 tablespoons butter

5 tablespoons thin honey

1 cup plain yogurt

1 large egg, at room temperature

grated rind of 1 lemon

¼ cup fresh lemon juice

1 cup all-purpose flour

1 cup whole-wheat flour

1½ teaspoons baking soda

⅛ teaspoon grated nutmeg

~ VARIATION ~

For Walnut Yogurt Honey Muffins, add ½ cup chopped walnuts, folded in with the flour. This makes a more substantial muffin.

---

1 Preheat the oven to 375°F. Grease a 12-cup muffin pan or use paper liners.

2 In a saucepan, melt the butter and honey. Remove from the heat and set aside to cool slightly.

3 ▲ In a bowl, whisk together the yogurt, egg, lemon rind and juice. Add the butter and honey mixture. Set aside.

4 ▲ In another bowl, sift together the dry ingredients.

5 Fold the dry ingredients into the yogurt mixture just to blend.

6 Fill the prepared cups two-thirds full. Bake until the tops spring back when touched lightly, 20–25 minutes. Let cool in the pan for 5 minutes before unmolding. Serve warm or at room temperature.

Blueberry Muffins

MAKES 12

1¼ cups flour
⅓ cup sugar
2 teaspoons baking powder
¼ teaspoon salt
2 eggs
4 tablespoons butter, melted
¾ cup milk
1 teaspoon vanilla extract
1 teaspoon grated lemon rind
1 cup fresh blueberries

1 Preheat the oven to 400°F.

2 ▼ Grease a 12-cup muffin pan or use paper liners.

3 ▲ Sift the flour, sugar, baking powder, and salt into a bowl.

4 In another bowl, whisk the eggs until blended. Add the melted butter, milk, vanilla, and lemon rind and stir to combine.

5 Make a well in the dry ingredients and pour in the egg mixture. With a large metal spoon, stir just until the flour is moistened, not until smooth.

6 ▲ Fold in the blueberries.

7 ▲ Spoon the batter into the cups, leaving room for the muffins to rise.

8 Bake until the tops spring back when touched lightly, 20–25 minutes. Let cool in the pan for 5 minutes before unmolding.

Apple Cranberry Muffins

MAKES 12

4 tablespoons butter or margarine
1 egg
½ cup sugar
grated rind of 1 large orange
½ cup fresh orange juice
1 cup flour
1 teaspoon baking powder
½ teaspoon baking soda
1 teaspoon ground cinnamon
½ teaspoon grated nutmeg
½ teaspoon ground allspice
¼ teaspoon ground ginger
¼ teaspoon salt
1–2 apples
1 cup cranberries
½ cup walnuts, chopped
confectioners' sugar, for dusting (optional)

1 Preheat the oven to 350°F. Grease a 12-cup muffin pan or use paper liners.

2 Melt the butter or margarine over gentle heat. Set aside to cool.

5 In a large bowl, sift together the flour, baking powder, baking soda, cinnamon, nutmeg, allspice, ginger, and salt. Set aside.

8 ▲ Add the apples, cranberries, and walnuts and stir to blend.

9 Fill the cups three-quarters full and bake until the tops spring back when touched lightly, 25–30 minutes. Transfer to a rack to cool. Dust with confectioners' sugar, if desired.

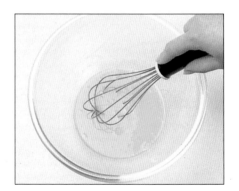

3 ▲ Place the egg in a mixing bowl and whisk lightly. Add the melted butter or margarine and whisk to combine.

4 Add the sugar, orange rind, and juice. Whisk to blend, then set aside.

6 ▲ Quarter, core, and peel the apples. With a sharp knife, chop in a coarse dice to obtain 1¼ cups.

7 Make a well in the dry ingredients and pour in the egg mixture. With a spoon, stir until just blended.

Chocolate Chip Muffins

MAKES 10

½ cup (1 stick) butter or margarine, at room temperature

⅓ cup granulated sugar

2 tablespoons dark brown sugar

2 eggs, at room temperature

1½ cups cake flour

1 teaspoon baking powder

½ cup milk

1 cup semisweet chocolate chips

1 Preheat the oven to 375°F. Grease 10 muffin cups or use paper liners.

2 ▼ With an electric mixer, cream the butter or margarine until soft. Add both sugars and beat until light and fluffy. Beat in the eggs, 1 at a time.

3 Sift together the flour and baking powder, twice. Fold into the butter mixture, alternating with the milk.

4 ▲ Divide half the mixture between the muffin cups. Sprinkle several chocolate chips on top, then cover with a spoonful of the batter. To ensure even baking, half-fill any empty cups with water.

5 Bake until lightly colored, about 25 minutes. Let stand 5 minutes before unmolding.

Chocolate Walnut Muffins

MAKES 12

¾ cup (1½ sticks) unsalted butter

4 1-ounce squares semisweet chocolate

1 1-ounce square unsweetened chocolate

1 cup granulated sugar

¼ cup dark brown sugar, firmly packed

4 eggs

1 teaspoon vanilla extract

¼ teaspoon almond extract

¾ cup flour

1 cup walnuts, chopped

1 Preheat the oven to 350°F. Grease a 12-cup muffin pan or use paper liners.

2 ▼ Melt the butter with the two chocolates in the top of a double boiler or in a heatproof bowl set over a pan of hot water. Transfer to a large mixing bowl.

3 Stir both the sugars into the chocolate mixture. Mix in the eggs, 1 at a time, then add the vanilla and almond extracts.

4 Sift over the flour and fold in.

5 ▲ Stir in the walnuts.

6 Fill the prepared cups almost to the top and bake until a cake tester inserted in the center barely comes out clean, 30–35 minutes. Let stand 5 minutes before transferring to a rack to cool completely.

Raisin Bran Muffins

MAKES 15

4 tablespoons butter or margarine
⅔ cup all-purpose flour
½ cup whole-wheat flour
1½ teaspoons baking soda
⅛ teaspoon salt
1 teaspoon ground cinnamon
½ cup bran
½ cup raisins
⅓ cup dark brown sugar, firmly packed
¼ cup granulated sugar
1 egg
1 cup buttermilk
juice of ½ lemon

1 Preheat the oven to 400°F. Grease 15 muffin cups or use paper liners.

2 ▲ Place the butter or margarine in a saucepan and melt over gentle heat. Set aside.

3 In a mixing bowl, sift together the all-purpose flour, whole-wheat flour, baking soda, salt, and cinnamon.

4 ▲ Add the bran, raisins, and sugars and stir until blended.

5 In another bowl, mix together the egg, buttermilk, lemon juice, and melted butter.

6 ▲ Add the buttermilk mixture to the dry ingredients and stir lightly and quickly just until moistened; do not mix until smooth.

7 ▲ Spoon the batter into the prepared muffin cups, filling them almost to the top. Half-fill any empty cups with water.

8 Bake until golden, 15–20 minutes. Serve warm or at room temperature.

Raspberry Crumble Muffins

MAKES 12

1½ cups flour

¼ cup granulated sugar

¼ cup light brown sugar, firmly packed

2 teaspoons baking powder

⅛ teaspoon salt

1 teaspoon ground cinnamon

½ cup (1 stick) butter, melted

1 egg

½ cup milk

1¼ cups fresh raspberries

grated rind of 1 lemon

FOR THE CRUMBLE TOPPING

¼ cup pecans, finely chopped

¼ cup dark brown sugar, firmly packed

3 tablespoons flour

1 teaspoon ground cinnamon

3 tablespoons butter, melted

1 Preheat the oven to 350°F. Grease a 12-cup muffin pan or use paper liners.

2 Sift the flour into a bowl. Add the sugars, baking powder, salt, and cinnamon and stir to blend.

3 ▲ Make a well in the center. Place the butter, egg, and milk in the well and mix until just combined. Stir in the raspberries and lemon rind. Spoon the batter into the prepared muffin cups, filling them almost to the top.

4 ▼ For the crumble topping, mix the pecans, dark brown sugar, flour, and cinnamon in a bowl. Add the melted butter and stir to blend.

5 ▲ Spoon some of the crumble over each muffin. Bake until browned, about 25 minutes. Transfer to a rack to cool slightly. Serve warm.

Carrot Muffins

MAKES 12

¾ cup margarine, at room temperature

½ cup dark brown sugar, firmly packed

1 egg, at room temperature

1 tablespoon water

2 cups grated carrots

1¼ cups flour

1 teaspoon baking powder

½ teaspoon baking soda

1 teaspoon ground cinnamon

¼ teaspoon grated nutmeg

½ teaspoon salt

1 Preheat the oven to 350°F. Grease a 12-cup muffin pan or use paper liners.

2 With an electric mixer, cream the margarine and sugar until light and fluffy. Beat in the egg and water.

3 ▲ Stir in the carrots.

4 Sift over the flour, baking powder, baking soda, cinnamon, nutmeg, and salt. Stir to blend.

5 ▼ Spoon the batter into the prepared muffin cups, filling them almost to the top. Bake until the tops spring back when touched lightly, about 35 minutes. Let stand 10 minutes before transferring to a rack.

Dried Cherry Muffins

MAKES 16

1 cup plain yogurt

1 cup dried cherries

½ cup (1 stick) butter, at room temperature

¾ cup sugar

2 eggs, at room temperature

1 teaspoon vanilla extract

1¾ cups flour

2 teaspoons baking powder

1 teaspoon baking soda

⅛ teaspoon salt

1 In a mixing bowl, combine the yogurt and cherries. Cover and let stand for 30 minutes.

2 Preheat the oven to 350°F. Grease 16 muffin cups or use paper liners.

3 With an electric mixer, cream the butter and sugar together until light and fluffy.

4 ▼ Add the eggs, 1 at a time, beating well after each addition. Add the vanilla and the cherry mixture and stir to blend. Set aside.

5 ▲ In another bowl, sift together the flour, baking powder, baking soda, and salt. Fold into the cherry mixture in 3 batches; do not overmix.

6 Fill the prepared cups two-thirds full. For even baking, half-fill any empty cups with water. Bake until the tops spring back when touched lightly, about 20 minutes. Transfer to a rack to cool.

Banana Muffins

MAKES 10

2 cups flour
1 teaspoon baking powder
1 teaspoon baking soda
¼ teaspoon salt
½ teaspoon ground cinnamon
¼ teaspoon grated nutmeg
3 large ripe bananas
1 egg
⅓ cup dark brown sugar, firmly packed
¼ cup vegetable oil
¼ cup raisins

1 Preheat the oven to 375°F.

2 ▼ Line 10 muffin cups with paper liners or grease.

3 Sift together the flour, baking powder, baking soda, salt, nutmeg, and cinnamon. Set aside.

4 ▲ With an electric mixer, beat the peeled bananas at moderate speed until mashed.

5 ▲ Beat in the egg, sugar, and oil.

6 Add the dry ingredients and beat in gradually, on low speed. Mix just until blended. With a wooden spoon, stir in the raisins.

7 Fill the prepared cups two-thirds full. For even baking, half-fill any empty cups with water.

8 ▲ Bake until the tops spring back when touched lightly, 20–25 minutes.

9 Transfer to a rack to cool.

Maple Pecan Muffins

MAKES 20

1¼ cups pecans
2½ cups flour
1 teaspoon baking powder
1 teaspoon baking soda
¼ teaspoon salt
¼ teaspoon ground cinnamon
½ cup granulated sugar
⅓ cup light brown sugar, firmly packed
3 tablespoons maple syrup
⅔ cup (10⅔ tablespoons) butter, at room temperature
3 eggs, at room temperature
1¼ cups buttermilk
60 pecan halves, for decorating

1 Preheat the oven to 350°F. Grease 2 12-cup muffin pans or use paper liners.

2 ▲ Spread the pecans on a baking sheet and toast in the oven for 5 minutes. When cool, chop coarsely and set aside.

~ **VARIATION** ~

For Pecan Spice Muffins, substitute an equal quantity of molasses for the maple syrup. Increase the cinnamon to ½ teaspoon, and add 1 teaspoon ground ginger and ½ teaspoon grated nutmeg, sifted with the flour and other dry ingredients.

3 In a bowl, sift together the flour, baking powder, baking soda, salt, and cinnamon. Set aside.

4 ▲ In a large mixing bowl, combine the granulated sugar, light brown sugar, maple syrup, and butter. Beat with an electric mixer until light and fluffy.

5 Add the eggs, 1 at a time, beating to incorporate thoroughly after each addition.

6 ▲ Pour half the buttermilk and half the dry ingredients into the butter mixture, then stir until blended. Repeat with the remaining buttermilk and dry ingredients.

7 Fold in the chopped pecans.

8 Fill the prepared cups two-thirds full. Top with the pecan halves. For even baking, half-fill any empty cup with water.

9 Bake until puffed up and golden, 20–25 minutes. Let stand 5 minutes before unmolding.

Oatmeal Buttermilk Muffins

MAKES 12

1 cup rolled oats
1 cup buttermilk
½ cup (1 stick) butter, at room temperature
½ cup dark brown sugar, firmly packed
1 egg, at room temperature
1 cup flour
1 teaspoon baking powder
½ teaspoon baking soda
¼ teaspoon salt
¼ cup raisins

~ **COOK'S TIP** ~

If buttermilk is not available, add 1 teaspoon lemon juice or vinegar per cup of milk. Let the mixture stand a few minutes to curdle.

1 ▲ In a bowl, combine the oats and buttermilk and let soak for 1 hour.

2 ▲ Grease a 12-cup muffin pan or use paper liners.

3 ▲ Preheat the oven to 400°F. With an electric mixer, cream the butter and sugar until light and fluffy. Beat in the egg.

4 In another bowl, sift together the flour, baking powder, baking soda, and salt. Stir into the butter mixture, alternating with the oat mixture. Fold in the raisins. Do not overmix.

5 Fill the prepared cups two-thirds full. Bake until a cake tester inserted in the center comes out clean, 20–25 minutes. Transfer to a rack to cool.

Pumpkin Muffins

MAKES 14

½ cup (1 stick) butter or margarine, at room temperature
¾ cup dark brown sugar, firmly packed
⅓ cup molasses
1 egg, at room temperature, beaten
1 cup cooked or canned pumpkin (about 8 ounces)
1¾ cups flour
¼ teaspoon salt
1 teaspoon baking soda
1½ teaspoons ground cinnamon
1 teaspoon grated nutmeg
¼ cup currants or raisins

1 Preheat the oven to 400°F. Grease 14 muffin cups or use paper liners.

2 With an electric mixer, cream the butter or margarine until soft. Add the sugar and molasses and beat until light and fluffy.

3 ▲ Add the egg and pumpkin and stir until well blended.

4 Sift over the flour, salt, baking soda, cinnnamon, and nutmeg. Fold just enough to blend; do not overmix.

5 ▼ Fold in the currants or raisins.

6 Spoon the batter into the prepared muffin cups, filling them three-quarters full.

7 Bake until the tops spring back when touched lightly, 12–15 minutes. Serve warm or cold.

Blackberry and Almond Muffins

MAKES 12

2½ cups plain unbleached flour

generous ¼ cup light brown sugar

4 teaspoons baking powder

pinch of salt

generous ½ cup chopped blanched
    almonds

generous ½ cup fresh blackberries

2 eggs

⅞ cup milk

4 tablespoons melted butter, plus a little
    more to grease cups, if using

1 tablespoon sloe gin

1 tablespoon rosewater

1 ▼ Mix the flour, brown sugar, baking powder and salt in a large bowl and stir in the almonds and blackberries, mixing them well to coat completely with the flour mixture. Preheat the oven to 400°F.

2 ▲ In another bowl, mix the eggs with the milk, then gradually add the butter, sloe gin and rosewater. Make a well in the center of the bowl of dry ingredients and add the egg and milk mixture. Stir well.

3 Spoon the mixture into a greased 12-cup muffin pan or cases. Bake for 20–25 minutes or until browned. Turn out the muffins on to a wire rack to cool. Serve with butter.

~ **COOK'S TIP** ~

Other berries can be substituted for the blackberries, such as raspberries or blueberries.

~ **VARIATION** ~

For Blackberry and Apple Muffins, substitute 2 dessert apples, peeled, cored, and diced, for the almonds. Add 1 teaspoon ground coriander to the flour mixture, and instead of the sloe gin and rosewater, substitute 2 tablespoons Crème de Cassis.

Cherry Marmalade Muffins

MAKES 12

2 cups self-rising flour
1 teaspoon apple pie spice
6 tablespoons sugar
½ cup candied cherries, quartered
2 tablespoons orange marmalade
⅔ cup skim milk
4 tablespoons soft sunflower margarine
marmalade, to brush

1 ▲ Preheat the oven to 400°F. Lightly grease a 12-cup muffin pan with oil.

2 ▲ Sift together the flour and spice, then stir in the sugar and cherries.

3 Mix the marmalade with the milk and beat into the dry ingredients with the margarine. Spoon into the greased cups. Bake for 20–25 minutes, until golden brown and firm.

4 ▼ Turn out on to a wire rack and brush the tops with warmed marmalade. Serve warm or cold.

~ **VARIATION** ~

To make Honey-Nut Lemon Muffins, substitute 2 tablespoons clear honey for the orange marmalade. Add the juice and grated rind of a lemon and ¼ cup toasted, chopped hazelnuts, instead of the candied cherries.

Banana-Pecan Muffins

MAKES 8

1¼ cups flour

1½ teaspoons baking powder

4 tablespoons butter or margarine, at room temperature

¾ cup sugar

1 egg

1 teaspoon vanilla extract

¾ cup mashed bananas (about 3 medium bananas)

½ cup pecans, chopped

⅓ cup milk

~ VARIATION ~

Use an equal quantity of walnuts instead of the pecans.

1 Preheat the oven to 375°F. Grease a muffin pan.

2 Sift the flour and baking powder into a small bowl. Set aside.

3 ▲ With an electric mixer, cream the butter or margarine and sugar together. Add the egg and vanilla and beat until fluffy. Mix in the banana.

4 ▼ Add the pecans. With the mixer on low speed, beat in the flour mixture alternately with the milk.

5 Spoon the batter into the prepared muffin cups, filling them two-thirds full. Bake until golden brown and a cake tester inserted into the center of a muffin comes out clean, 20–25 minutes.

6 Let cool in the pan on a wire rack for 10 minutes. To loosen, run a knife gently around each muffin and unmold onto the wire rack. Let cool 10 minutes longer before serving.

Blueberry-Cinnamon Muffins

MAKES 8

1 cup flour

1 tablespoon baking powder

⅛ teaspoon salt

⅓ cup light brown sugar, firmly packed

1 egg

¾ cup milk

3 tablespoons corn oil

2 teaspoons ground cinnamon

1 cup fresh or thawed frozen blueberries

1 Preheat the oven to 375°F. Grease a muffin pan.

2 With an electric mixer, beat the first 8 ingredients together until smooth.

3 ▲ Fold in the blueberries.

4 ▲ Spoon the batter into the muffin cups, filling them two-thirds full. Bake until a cake tester inserted in the center of a muffin comes out clean, about 25 minutes.

5 Let cool in the pan on a wire rack for 10 minutes, then unmold the muffins onto the wire rack and allow to cool completely.

Raspberry Muffins

MAKES 10–12

1 cup self-rising flour

1 cup whole-wheat self-rising flour

3 tablespoons sugar

½ teaspoon salt

2 eggs, beaten

scant 1 cup milk

4 tablespoons melted butter

6 oz raspberries, fresh or frozen
(defrosted for less than 30 minutes)

1 ▼ Preheat the oven to 375°F. Lightly grease the muffin pan, or use paper liners. Sift both the flours, sugar and the salt together, then tip back in the whole-wheat flakes from the sifter.

2 ▲ Beat the eggs, milk and butter with the dry ingredients to give a thick batter. Add the raspberries.

3 ▲ Stir in the raspberries gently. (If you are using frozen raspberries, work quickly as the cold berries make the mixture solidify.) If you mix too much the raspberries begin to disintegrate and color the dough. Spoon the mixture into the tins or paper cases.

4 Bake the muffins for 30 minutes, until well risen and just firm. Serve warm or cool.

Blueberry-Vanilla Muffins

MAKES 12

3 cups flour
2 teaspoons baking powder
¼ teaspoon salt
½ cup sugar
2 eggs, beaten
1¼ cups milk
½ cup butter, melted
1 teaspoon vanilla extract
1⅓ cups blueberries

1 Preheat the oven to 400°F. Grease a 12-cup muffin pan.

2 Sift the flour, baking powder and salt into a large mixing bowl and stir in the sugar.

3 ▲ Place the eggs, milk, butter and vanilla extract in a separate bowl and whisk together well.

4 ▲ Fold the egg mixture into the dry ingredients with a metal spoon, then gently stir in the blueberries.

5 Spoon the mixture into the muffin cups, filling them until just below the top. Place the muffin pan on the top shelf of the oven and bake for 20–25 minutes, until the muffins are well risen and lightly browned. Leave the muffins in the pan for 5 minutes and then turn them out on to a wire rack to cool. Serve warm or cold.

~ **COOK'S TIP** ~

Fresh blueberries are best for this recipe, but if you can't find them, use frozen ones instead. Just add them to the batter without thawing first.

Sweet
Quick Breads

When there's no time to make yeasted bread, baking
quick breads can be equally satisfying. Old favorites
include Banana and Oat Gingerbread, or try the more
unusual Sweet Potato and Raisin Bread, or Zucchini
Walnut Loaf. These versatile breads can be served
with fresh fruit for an unusual dessert, or just toasted
and spread with butter and jam.

Whole-Wheat Banana Nut Bread

MAKES 1 LOAF

½ cup (1 stick) butter, at room temperature

½ cup granulated sugar

2 eggs, at room temperature

1 cup all-purpose flour

1 teaspoon baking soda

¼ teaspoon salt

1 teaspoon ground cinnamon

½ cup whole-wheat flour

3 large ripe bananas

1 teaspoon vanilla extract

½ cup pecans, chopped

1 Preheat the oven to 350°F. Line the bottom and sides of a 9- × 5-inch loaf pan with wax paper and grease.

2 With an electric mixer, cream the butter and sugar together until light and fluffy.

3 ▲ Add the eggs, 1 at a time, beating well after each addition.

4 Sift the all-purpose flour, baking soda, salt, and cinnamon over the butter mixture and stir to blend.

5 ▲ Stir in the whole-wheat flour.

6 ▲ With a fork, mash the bananas to a purée, then stir into the batter. Stir in the vanilla and pecans.

7 ▲ Pour the batter into the prepared pan and spread level.

8 Bake until a cake tester inserted in the center comes out clean, 50–60 minutes. Let stand 10 minutes before transferring to a rack.

Sweet Potato and Raisin Bread

MAKES 1 LOAF

2½ cups flour
2 teaspoons baking powder
½ teaspoon salt
1 teaspoon ground cinnamon
½ teaspoon grated nutmeg
2 cups mashed cooked sweet potatoes (about 1 pound)
½ cup light brown sugar, firmly packed
½ cup (1 stick) butter or margarine, melted and cooled
3 eggs, beaten
½ cup raisins

1 ▼ Preheat oven to 350°F. Grease a 9- × 5-inch loaf pan.

2 Sift the flour, baking powder, salt, cinnamon, and nutmeg into a small bowl. Set aside.

3 ▼ With an electric mixer, beat the mashed sweet potatoes with the brown sugar, butter or margarine, and eggs until well mixed.

4 ▼ Add the flour mixture and the raisins. Stir with a wooden spoon until the flour is just mixed in.

5 ▲ Transfer the batter to the prepared pan. Bake until a cake tester inserted in the center comes out clean, 1–1¼ hours.

6 Let cool in the pan on a wire rack for 15 minutes, then unmold the bread from the pan onto the wire rack and let cool completely.

Zucchini-Walnut Loaf

MAKES 1 LOAF

3 eggs

⅓ cup light brown sugar, firmly packed

½ cup sunflower oil

2 cups whole-wheat flour

1 teaspoon baking powder

1 teaspoon baking soda

1 teaspoon ground cinnamon

¾ teaspoon ground allspice

½ tablespoon green cardamoms, seeds removed and crushed

2 cups zucchini, coarsely grated

½ cup walnuts, chopped

¼ cup sunflower seeds

1 ▲ Preheat the oven to 350°F. Line the base and sides of a 2 lb loaf pan with parchment paper.

2 ▲ Beat the eggs and sugar together and gradually add the oil.

3 ▲ Sift the whole-wheat flour into a large bowl, together with the baking powder, baking soda, cinnamon and allspice.

4 ▲ Mix into the egg mixture with the rest of the ingredients, reserving 1 tablespoon of the sunflower seeds for the top.

5 ▲ Spoon into the loaf pan, level off the top, and sprinkle with the reserved sunflower seeds.

6 ▲ Bake for 1 hour or until a skewer inserted in the center comes out clean. Leave to cool slightly before turning out onto a wire rack to cool completely.

~ **VARIATION** ~

For Spinach-Walnut Loaf, use ½ pound chopped, cooked spinach instead of the zucchini. Substitute ¼ teaspoon freshly grated nutmeg for the cardamoms, and sesame seeds for the sunflower seeds. Stir ¼ cup grated Parmesan or Cheddar cheese into the mixture.

Cranberry Orange Bread

MAKES 1 LOAF

2 cups flour

½ cup sugar

1 tablespoon baking powder

½ teaspoon salt

grated rind of 1 large orange

⅔ cup fresh orange juice

2 eggs, lightly beaten

6 tablespoons butter or margarine, melted

1¼ cups fresh cranberries

½ cup walnuts, chopped

1 Preheat the oven to 350°F. Line the bottom and sides of a 9- × 5-inch loaf pan with wax paper and grease.

2 Sift the flour, sugar, baking powder, and salt into a mixing bowl.

3 ▼ Stir in the orange rind.

4 ▲ Make a well in the center and add the orange juice, eggs, and melted butter or margarine. Stir from the center until the ingredients are blended; do not overmix.

5 ▲ Add the cranberries and walnuts and stir until blended.

6 Transfer the batter to the prepared pan and bake until a cake tester inserted in the center comes out clean, 45–50 minutes.

7 ▲ Let cool in the pan for 10 minutes before transferring to a rack to cool completely. Serve thinly sliced, toasted or plain, with butter or cream cheese, and jam.

Date-Nut Bread

MAKES 1 LOAF

1 cup pitted dates, chopped
¾ cup boiling water
4 tablespoons unsalted butter, at room temperature
¼ cup dark brown sugar, firmly packed
¼ cup granulated sugar
1 egg, at room temperature
2 tablespoons brandy
1⅓ cups flour
2 teaspoons baking powder
½ teaspoon salt
¾ teaspoon freshly grated nutmeg
¾ cup pecans, coarsely chopped

1 ▲ Place the dates in a bowl and pour over the boiling water. Set aside to cool.

2 Preheat the oven to 350°F. Line the bottom and sides of a 9- × 5-inch loaf pan with wax paper and grease.

3 ▲ With an electric mixer, cream the butter and sugars until light and fluffy. Beat in the egg and brandy, then set aside.

4 Sift the flour, baking powder, salt, and nutmeg together, 3 times.

5 ▼ Fold the dry ingredients into the sugar mixture in 3 batches, alternating with the dates and water.

6 ▲ Fold in the pecans.

7 Pour the batter into the prepared pan and bake until a cake tester inserted in the center comes out clean, 45–50 minutes. Let cool in the pan for 10 minutes before transferring to a rack to cool completely.

Blueberry Streusel Bread

MAKES 8 PIECES

4 tablespoons butter or margarine, at room temperature
¾ cup sugar
1 egg, at room temperature
½ cup milk
2 cups flour
2 teaspoons baking powder
½ teaspoon salt
2 cups fresh blueberries
FOR THE TOPPING
½ cup sugar
⅓ cup flour
½ teaspoon ground cinnamon
4 tablespoons butter, cut in pieces

1 Preheat the oven to 375°F. Grease a 9-inch square baking dish.

2 With an electric mixer, cream the butter or margarine with the sugar until light and fluffy. Add the egg, beat to combine, then mix in the milk until blended.

3 ▼ Sift over the flour, baking powder, and salt and stir just enough to blend the ingredients.

4 ▲ Add the blueberries and stir.

5 Transfer to the baking dish.

6 ▲ For the topping, place the sugar, flour, cinnamon, and butter in a mixing bowl. Cut in with a pastry blender until the mixture resembles coarse crumbs.

7 ▲ Sprinkle the topping over the batter in the pan.

8 Bake until a cake tester inserted in the center comes out clean, about 45 minutes. Serve warm or cold.

Dried Fruit Loaf

2½ cups mixed dried fruit, such as currants, raisins, chopped dried apricots, and dried cherries

1¼ cups cold strong tea

1 cup dark brown sugar, firmly packed

grated rind and juice of 1 small orange

grated rind and juice of 1 lemon

1 egg, lightly beaten

1¾ cups flour

1 tablespoon baking powder

⅛ teaspoon salt

1 ▲ In a bowl, toss together all the dried fruit, pour over the tea, and leave to soak overnight.

2 Preheat the oven to 350°F. Line the bottom and sides of a 9- × 5-inch loaf pan with wax paper and grease.

3 ▲ Strain the fruit, reserving the liquid. In a bowl, combine the sugar, orange and lemon rind, and fruit.

4 ▼ Pour the orange and lemon juice into a measuring cup; if the quantity is less than 1 cup, complete with the soaking liquid.

5 Stir the citrus juices and egg into the dried fruit mixture.

6 In another bowl, sift together the flour, baking powder, and salt. Stir into the fruit mixture until blended.

7 Transfer to the prepared pan and bake until a cake tester inserted in the center comes out clean, about 1¼ hours. Let stand 10 minutes before unmolding.

Lemon Walnut Bread

MAKES 1 LOAF

½ cup (1 stick) butter or margarine, at
   room temperature

½ cup sugar

2 eggs, at room temperature, separated

grated rind of 2 lemons

2 tablespoons fresh lemon juice

1½ cups cake flour

2 teaspoons baking powder

½ cup milk

½ cup walnuts, chopped

⅛ teaspooon salt

1 Preheat the oven to 350°F. Line
the bottom and sides of a 9- × 5-inch
loaf pan with wax paper and grease.

2 With an electric mixer, cream the
butter or margarine with the sugar
until light and fluffy.

3 ▲ Beat in the egg yolks.

4 Add the lemon rind and juice and
stir until blended. Set aside.

5 ▲ In another bowl, sift together
the flour and baking powder, 3 times.
Fold into the butter mixture in 3
batches, alternating with the milk.
Fold in the walnuts. Set aside.

6 ▲ Beat the egg whites and salt
until stiff peaks form. Fold a large
dollop of the egg whites into the
walnut mixture to lighten it. Fold in
the remaining egg whites carefully just
until blended.

7 ▲ Pour the batter into the
prepared pan and bake until a cake
tester inserted in the center of the loaf
comes out clean, 45–50 minutes. Let
stand 5 minutes before unmolding
onto a rack to cool completely.

Apricot Nut Loaf

MAKES 1 LOAF

¾ cup dried apricots
1 large orange
½ cup raisins
⅔ cup sugar
⅓ cup oil
2 eggs, lightly beaten
2¼ cups flour
2 teaspoons baking powder
½ teaspoon salt
1 teaspoon baking soda
½ cup walnuts, chopped

1 Preheat the oven to 350°F. Line the bottom and sides of a 9- × 5-inch loaf pan with wax paper and grease.

2 Place the apricots in a bowl and add lukewarm water to cover. Let stand for 30 minutes.

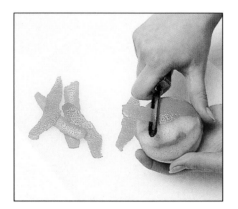

3 ▲ With a vegetable peeler, remove the orange rind, leaving the pith.

4 With a sharp knife, finely chop the orange rind strips.

5 Drain the apricots and chop coarsely. Place in a bowl with the orange rind and raisins. Set aside.

6 Squeeze the peeled orange. Measure the juice and add enough hot water to obtain ¾ cup liquid.

7 ▼ Pour the orange juice mixture over the apricot mixture. Stir in the sugar, oil, and eggs. Set aside.

8 In another bowl, sift together the flour, baking powder, salt, and baking soda. Fold the flour mixture into the apricot mixture in 3 batches.

9 ▲ Stir in the walnuts.

10 Spoon the batter into the prepared pan and bake until a cake tester inserted in the center comes out clean, 55–60 minutes. If the loaf browns too quickly, protect the top with a sheet of foil. Let cool in the pan for 10 minutes before transferring to a rack to cool completely.

Orange Honey Bread

MAKES 1 LOAF

2½ cups flour

2½ teaspoons baking powder

½ teaspoon baking soda

½ teaspoon salt

2 tablespoons margarine

1 cup thin honey

1 egg, at room temperature, lightly
  beaten

1½ tablespoons grated orange rind

¾ cup freshly squeezed orange juice

¾ cup walnuts, chopped

1 Preheat the oven to 325°F.

2 Sift together the flour, baking
powder, baking soda, and salt.

3 Line the bottom and sides of a
9- × 5-inch loaf pan with wax paper
and grease.

4 ▲ With an electric mixer, cream
the margarine until soft. Stir in the
honey until blended, then stir in the
egg. Add the orange rind and stir to
combine thoroughly.

5 ▲ Fold the flour mixture into the
honey and egg mixture in 3 batches,
alternating with the orange juice. Stir
in the walnuts.

6 Pour into the pan and bake until a
cake tester inserted in the center
comes out clean, 60–70 minutes. Let
stand 10 minutes before unmolding
onto a rack to cool.

Applesauce Bread

MAKES 1 LOAF

1 egg

1 cup applesauce

4 tablespoons butter or margarine,
  melted

½ cup dark brown sugar, firmly packed

¼ cup granulated sugar

2 cups flour

2 teaspoons baking powder

½ teaspoon baking soda

½ teaspoon salt

1 teaspoon ground cinnamon

½ teaspoon grated nutmeg

½ cup currants or raisins

½ cup pecans, chopped

1 Preheat the oven to 350°F. Line
the bottom and sides of a 9- × 5-inch
loaf pan with wax paper and grease.

2 ▲ Break the egg into a bowl and
beat lightly. Stir in the applesauce,
butter or margarine, and both sugars.
Set aside.

3 In another bowl, sift together the
flour, baking powder, baking soda,
salt, cinnamon, and nutmeg. Fold dry
ingredients into the applesauce
mixture in 3 batches.

4 ▼ Stir in the currants or raisins,
and pecans.

5 Pour into the prepared pan and
bake until a cake tester inserted in the
center comes out clean, about 1 hour.
Let stand 10 minutes before
unmolding and transferring to a
cooling rack.

Glazed Banana Spice Loaf

MAKES 1 LOAF

1 large ripe banana

½ cup (1 stick) butter, at room temperature

¾ cup granulated sugar

2 eggs, at room temperature

1½ cups flour

1 teaspoon salt

1 teaspoon baking soda

½ teaspoon grated nutmeg

¼ teaspoon ground allspice

¼ teaspoon ground cloves

¾ cup sour cream

1 teaspoon vanilla extract

FOR THE GLAZE

1 cup confectioners' sugar

1–2 tablespoons fresh lemon juice

1 Preheat the oven to 350°F. Line an 8½- × 4½-inch loaf pan with wax paper and grease.

2 ▼ With a fork, mash the banana in a bowl. Set aside.

3 With an electric mixer, cream the butter and sugar until light and fluffy. Add the eggs, 1 at a time, beating to blend well after each addition.

4 Sift together the flour, salt, baking soda, nutmeg, allspice, and cloves. Add to the butter mixture and stir to combine well.

5 ▲ Add the sour cream, banana, and vanilla and mix just enough to blend. Pour into the prepared pan.

6 ▲ Bake until the top springs back when touched lightly, 45–50 minutes. Let cool in the pan for 10 minutes before unmolding.

7 ▲ For the glaze, combine the confectioners' sugar and lemon juice, then stir until smooth.

8 To glaze, place the cooled loaf on a rack set over a baking sheet. Pour the glaze over the top of the bread and allow to set.

Chocolate Chip Walnut Loaf

MAKES 1 LOAF

½ cup granulated sugar

¾ cup cake flour

1 teaspoon baking powder

4 tablespoons potato flour or cornstarch

9 tablespoons butter, at room temperature

2 eggs, at room temperature

1 teaspoon vanilla extract

2 tablespoons currants or raisins

¼ cup walnuts, finely chopped

grated rind of ½ lemon

¼ cup semisweet chocolate chips

confectioners' sugar, for dusting

1 Preheat the oven to 350°F. Line an 8½- × 4½-inch loaf pan with wax paper and grease.

2 ▲ Sprinkle 1½ tablespoons of the granulated sugar into the pan and tilt to distribute the sugar in an even layer over the bottom and sides. Shake out any excess.

~ **COOK'S TIP** ~

For best results, the eggs should be at room temperature. If they are too cold when folded into the creamed butter mixture, it may separate. If this happens, add a spoonful of the flour to help stabilize the mixture.

3 ▼ Sift together the cake flour, baking powder, and potato flour or cornstarch, 3 times. Set aside.

4 With an electric mixer, cream the butter until soft. Add the remaining sugar and continue beating until light and fluffy. Add the eggs, 1 at a time, beating to incorporate thoroughly after each addition.

5 Gently fold the dry ingredients into the butter mixture, in 3 batches; do not overmix.

6 ▲ Fold in the vanilla, currants or raisins, walnuts, lemon rind, and chocolate chips until just blended.

7 Pour the batter into the prepared pan and bake until a cake tester inserted in the center comes out clean, 45–50 minutes. Let cool in the pan for 5 minutes before transferring to a rack to cool completely. Dust over an even layer of confectioners' sugar before serving.

Date and Nut Loaf

MAKES 2 × 1 LB LOAVES

2 cups flour

2 cups whole-wheat flour

1 teaspoon salt

6 tablespoons brown sugar

1 package dried fast-action yeast

4 tablespoons butter or margarine

1 tablespoon molasses

4 tablespoons malt extract

1 cup lukewarm milk

½ cup chopped dates

½ cup chopped nuts

½ cup golden raisins

½ cup raisins

2 tablespoons honey, to glaze

1 Sift the flours and salt into a large bowl, then tip in the wheat flakes that are caught in the sifter. Stir in the sugar and yeast.

2 ▲ Put the butter or margarine in a small pan with the molasses and malt extract. Stir over a low heat until melted. Leave to cool, then combine with the milk.

3 Stir the liquid into the dry ingredients and knead thoroughly for 15 minutes until the dough is elastic. (If you have a dough blade on your food processor, follow the manufacturer's instructions for timings.)

4 ▲ Knead in the fruits and nuts. Transfer the dough to an oiled bowl, cover with plastic wrap and leave in a warm place for about 1½ hours, until the dough has doubled in size.

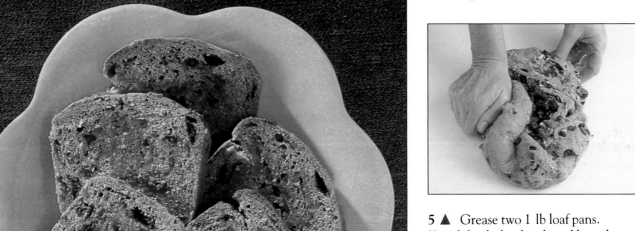

5 ▲ Grease two 1 lb loaf pans. Knock back the dough and knead lightly. Divide in half, form into loaves and place in the pans. Cover and leave in a warm place for about 30 minutes, until risen. Meanwhile, preheat the oven to 375°F.

6 Bake for 35–40 minutes, until well risen and sounding hollow when tapped underneath. Cool on a wire rack. Brush with honey while warm.

Gingerbread

SERVES 8–10

1 tablespoon vinegar
¾ cup milk
1½ cups flour
2 teaspoons baking powder
¼ teaspoon baking soda
½ teaspoon salt
2 teaspoons ground ginger
1 teaspoon ground cinnamon
¼ teaspoon ground cloves
½ cup (1 stick) butter, at room temperature
½ cup sugar
1 egg, at room temperature
¾ cup molasses
whipped cream, for serving
chopped stem ginger, for decorating

1 ▲ Preheat the oven to 350°F. Line the bottom of a shallow 8-inch square cake pan with wax paper or nonstick baking parchment. Grease the paper and sides of the pan.

2 ▲ Add the vinegar to the milk and set aside. It will curdle.

3 In another mixing bowl, sift all the dry ingredients together 3 times and set aside.

4 With an electric mixer, cream the butter and sugar until light and fluffy. Beat in the egg until well combined.

5 ▼ Stir in the molasses.

6 ▲ Fold in the dry ingredients in 4 batches, alternating with the curdled milk. Mix only enough to blend.

7 Pour into the prepared pan and bake until firm, 45–50 minutes. Cut into squares and serve warm, with whipped cream. Decorate with the stem ginger.

Mango Bread

MAKES 2 LOAVES

2 cups flour

2 teaspoons baking soda

2 teaspoons ground cinnamon

½ teaspoon salt

½ cup margarine, at room temperature

3 eggs, at room temperature

1½ cups sugar

½ cup vegetable oil

2 cups chopped ripe mangoes (about 2–3 mangoes)

¾ cup shredded coconut

½ cup raisins

1 Preheat the oven to 350°F. Line the bottom and sides of 2 9- × 5-inch loaf pans with wax paper and grease.

2 Sift together the flour, baking soda, cinnamon, and salt. Set aside.

3 With an electric mixer, cream the margarine until soft.

4 ▼ Beat in the eggs and sugar until light and fluffy. Beat in the oil.

5 Fold the dry ingredients into the creamed ingredients in 3 batches.

6 Fold in the mangoes, ½ cup of the coconut, and the raisins.

7 ▲ Spoon the batter into the pans.

8 Sprinkle over the remaining coconut. Bake until a cake tester inserted in the center comes out clean, 50–60 minutes. Let stand for 10 minutes before transferring to a rack to cool completely.

Zucchini Bread

MAKES 1 LOAF

4 tablespoons butter

3 eggs

1 cup corn oil

1½ cups sugar

2 cups grated unpeeled zucchini

2 cups flour

2 teaspoons baking soda

1 teaspoon baking powder

1 teaspoon salt

1 teaspoon ground cinnamon

1 teaspoon grated nutmeg

¼ teaspoon ground cloves

1 cup walnuts, chopped

1 Preheat the oven to 350°F. Line the bottom and sides of a 9- × 5-inch loaf pan with wax paper and grease.

2 ▲ In a saucepan, melt the butter over low heat. Set aside.

3 With an electric mixer, beat the eggs and oil together until thick. Beat in the sugar. Stir in the melted butter and zucchini. Set aside.

4 ▲ In another bowl, sift all the dry ingredients together 3 times. Carefully fold into the zucchini mixture. Fold in the walnuts.

5 Pour into the pan and bake until a cake tester inserted in the center comes out clean, 60–70 minutes. Let stand 10 minutes before unmolding.

Pineapple and Apricot Bread

SERVES 10–12

¾ cup sweet butter

¾ cup sugar

3 eggs, beaten

few drops vanilla extract

2 cups cake flour, sifted

¼ teaspoon salt

1½ teaspoons baking powder

1⅓ cups ready-to-eat dried apricots, chopped

½ cup each chopped crystallized ginger and crystallized pineapple

grated rind and juice of ½ orange

grated rind and juice of ½ lemon

a little milk

1 ▲ Preheat the oven to 350°F. Double line an 8-inch round or 7-inch square cake pan. Cream the butter and sugar together until light and fluffy.

2 Gradually beat the eggs into the creamed mixture with the vanilla extract, beating well after each addition. Sift together the flour, salt and baking powder, and add a little with the last of the egg, then fold in the rest.

3 ▲ Fold in the fruit, crystallized fruits and fruit rinds gently, then add sufficient fruit juice and milk to give a fairly soft dropping consistency.

4 ▲ Spoon into the prepared pan and smooth the top with a wet spoon. Bake for 20 minutes, then reduce the heat to 325°F for a further 1½–2 hours, or until firm to the touch and a skewer comes out of the center clean. Leave the cake to cool in the pan, turn out and wrap in fresh paper before storing in an airtight tin.

~ **COOK'S TIP** ~

This is not a long-keeping cake, but it does freeze, well-wrapped in wax paper and then foil.

Banana Bread

MAKES 1 LOAF

1½ cups flour
2¼ teaspoons baking powder
½ teaspoon salt
¾ teaspoon ground cinnamon (optional)
¼ cup wheat germ
5 tablespoons butter, at room temperature, or ⅓ cup shortening
⅔ cup sugar
¾ teaspoon grated lemon rind
1¼ cups mashed ripe bananas (2–3 bananas)
2 eggs, beaten to mix

1 Preheat the oven to 350°F. Grease and flour an 8½- × 4½-inch loaf pan.

2 ▲ Sift the flour, baking powder, salt, and cinnamon, if using, into a bowl. Stir in the wheat germ.

3 ▲ In another bowl, beat the butter or shortening with the sugar and lemon rind until the mixture is light and fluffy.

4 ▲ Add the mashed bananas and eggs and mix well.

5 Add the dry ingredients and blend quickly and evenly.

~ **VARIATION** ~

For Banana Walnut Bread, add ½–¾ cup finely chopped walnuts with the dry ingredients.

6 ▼ Spoon into the prepared loaf pan. Bake until a wooden skewer inserted in the center comes out clean, about 1 hour.

7 Let the bread cool in the pan about 5 minutes, then unmould onto a wire rack to cool completely.

Banana-Orange Loaf

MAKES 1 LOAF

¾ cup whole-wheat flour

¾ cup flour

1 teaspoon baking powder

1 teaspoon apple pie spice

3 tablespoons slivered hazelnuts, toasted

2 large ripe bananas

1 egg

2 tablespoons sunflower oil

2 tablespoons clear honey

finely grated rind and juice 1 small
    orange

4 orange slices, halved

2 teaspoons confectioners' sugar

1 ▼ Preheat the oven to 350°F. Brush a 4-cup loaf pan with sunflower oil and line the base with nonstick baking paper.

2 ▲ Sift the flours with the baking powder and spice into a large bowl, adding any bran that is caught in the sifter. Stir the hazelnuts into the dry ingredients.

3 ▲ Peel and mash the bananas. Beat in the egg, oil, honey, and the orange rind and juice. Stir evenly into the dry ingredients.

4 Spoon into the prepared pan and smooth the top. Bake for 40–45 minutes, or until firm and golden brown. Turn out and cool on a wire rack.

5 Sprinkle the orange slices with the confectioners' sugar and broil until golden. Use to decorate the cake.

~ COOK'S TIP ~

If you plan to keep the loaf for more than three days, omit the orange slices, brush with honey and sprinkle with flaked hazelnuts.

Spiced Date and Walnut Bread

MAKES 1 LOAF

2½ cups whole-wheat self-rising flour

2 teaspoons apple pie spice

¾ cup chopped dates

½ cup chopped walnuts

4 tablespoons sunflower oil

½ cup brown sugar

1¼ cups skim milk

walnut halves, to decorate

1 Preheat the oven to 350°F. Grease and line a 2 lb loaf pan with nonstick baking paper.

2 ▲ Sift together the flour and spice, returning any bran from the sifter. Stir in the dates and walnuts.

3 ▲ Mix the oil, sugar, and milk, then stir evenly into the dry ingredients.

4 ▲ Spoon into the prepared pan and arrange the walnut halves on top.

5 Bake the bread in the oven for about 45–50 minutes, or until golden brown and firm. Turn out the bread, remove the baking paper and leave to cool on a wire rack.

~ COOK'S TIP ~

Pecans can be used in place of the walnuts in this bread.

Banana and Oat Gingerbread

MAKES 1 LOAF

1¾ cups flour

2 teaspoons baking soda

2 teaspoons ground ginger

1¾ cups oatmeal

4 tablespoons brown sugar

6 tablespoons sunflower margarine

⅔ cup corn syrup

1 egg, beaten

3 ripe bananas, mashed

¾ cup confectioners' sugar

preserved ginger, to decorate

1 Preheat the oven to 325°F. Grease and line a 7- × 11-inch cake pan.

2 ▼ Sift together the flour, baking soda, and ginger, then stir in the oatmeal. Melt the sugar, margarine, and syrup in a saucepan, then stir into the flour mixture. Beat in the egg and mashed bananas.

3 ▲ Spoon into the pan and bake for about 1 hour, or until firm to the touch. Allow to cool in the pan, then turn out and cut into squares.

4 ▲ Sift the confectioners' sugar into a bowl and stir in just enough water to make a smooth, runny icing. Drizzle the icing over each square and top with a piece of preserved ginger, if you like.

~ COOK'S TIP ~

This is a nutritious, energy-giving cake that is a good choice for lunch boxes as it doesn't break up too easily. This gingerbread keeps well, stored in a covered container for up to 2 months.

Fruit Loaf

MAKES 1

¾ cup coarsely chopped mixed dried fruit, such as apples, apricots, prunes and peaches

1 cup hot tea

2 cups whole-wheat self-rising flour

1 teaspoon grated nutmeg

4 tablespoons brown sugar

3 tablespoons sunflower oil

3 tablespoons skim milk

raw sugar, to sprinkle

1 ▲ Soak the dried fruits in the tea for several hours or overnight. Drain and reserve the liquid.

2 Preheat the oven to 350°F. Thoroughly grease a deep 7-inch round cake pan and line the base with nonstick baking paper.

3 ▲ Sift the flour into a bowl with the nutmeg. Stir in the brown sugar, fruit, and tea. Add the oil and milk and mix well.

4 ▼ Spoon the mixture into the prepared pan and sprinkle with raw sugar. Bake for 50–55 minutes or until firm. Turn out and cool on a wire rack.

~ **VARIATION** ~

For Tropical Fruit Loaf, substitute dried mango, papaya, and pineapple for the dried fruit mixture, and dark rum instead of the skim milk. Make in an 8-in loaf pan instead of the round cake pan.

Fruit and Bourbon Bread

MAKES 1 LOAF

1½ cups walnuts, chopped
½ cup raisins, chopped
½ cup currants
1 cup flour
1 teaspoon baking powder
¼ teaspoon salt
½ cup (1 stick) butter
1 cup sugar
3 eggs, at room temperature, separated
1 teaspoon grated nutmeg
½ teaspoon ground cinnamon
⅓ cup bourbon whiskey
confectioners' sugar, for dusting

1 ▼ Preheat the oven to 325°F. Line the bottom of a 9- × 5- × 3-inch loaf pan with wax paper and grease the paper and sides of the pan.

2 ▲ Place the walnuts, raisins, and currants in a bowl. Sprinkle over 2 tablespoons of the flour, mix and set aside. Sift together the remaining flour, baking powder, and salt.

3 ▲ Cream the butter and sugar until light and fluffy. Beat in the egg yolks.

4 Mix the nutmeg, cinnamon, and whiskey. Fold into the butter mixture, alternating with the flour mixture.

5 ▲ In another bowl, beat the egg whites until stiff. Fold into the whiskey mixture until just blended. Fold in the walnut mixture.

6 Bake until a cake tester inserted in the center comes out clean, about 1 hour. Let cool in the pan. Dust with confectioners' sugar over a template.

Sweet Sesame Loaf

MAKES 1 OR 2 LOAVES

⅔ cup sesame seeds

2 cups flour

2½ teaspoons baking powder

1 teaspoon salt

4 tablespoons butter or margarine, at room temperature

⅔ cup sugar

2 eggs, at room temperature

grated rind of 1 lemon

1½ cups milk

1 Preheat the oven to 350°F. Line a 10- × 6-inch baking pan, or 2 small loaf pans, with wax paper and grease.

2 ▲ Reserve 2 tablespoons of the sesame seeds. Spread the rest on a baking sheet and bake until lightly toasted, about 10 minutes.

3 Sift the flour, salt, and baking powder into a bowl.

4 ▲ Stir in the toasted sesame seeds and set aside.

5 With an electric mixer, cream the butter or margarine and sugar together until light and fluffy. Beat in the eggs, then stir in the lemon rind and milk.

6 ▼ Pour the milk mixture over the dry ingredients and fold in with a large metal spoon until just blended.

7 ▲ Pour into the pan and sprinkle over the reserved sesame seeds.

8 Bake until a cake tester inserted in the center comes out clean, about 1 hour. Let cool in the pan for 10 minutes before unmolding.

SAVORY
MUFFINS & BREADS

Quick and easy to make, light, fragrant muffins and
breads are ideal for packed lunches, brunches or picnics.
Use Rosemary Focaccia to make a satisfying sandwich
with an Italian flavor, and serve Tomato or
Italian Bread Sticks with soups and stews.
Try Bacon and Cornmeal Muffins – packed with
protein for a fortifying breakfast.

Cheese Muffins

MAKES 9

4 tablespoons butter

1½ cups flour

2 teaspoons baking powder

2 tablespoons sugar

¼ teaspoon salt

1 teaspoon paprika

2 eggs

½ cup milk

1 teaspoon dried thyme

2 ounces sharp Cheddar cheese, cut into
   ½-inch dice

1 Preheat the oven to 375°F. Thickly grease 9 muffin cups or use paper liners.

2 Melt the butter and set aside.

3 ▼ In a mixing bowl, sift together the flour, baking powder, sugar, salt, and paprika.

4 ▲ In another bowl, combine the eggs, milk, melted butter, and thyme, and whisk to blend.

5 Add the milk mixture to the dry ingredients and stir just until moistened; do not mix until smooth.

6 ▲ Place a heaped spoonful of batter into the prepared cups. Drop a few pieces of cheese over each, then top with another spoonful of batter. For even baking, half-fill any empty muffin cups with water.

7 ▲ Bake until puffed and golden, about 25 minutes. Let stand 5 minutes before unmolding onto a rack. Serve warm or at room temperature.

Bacon Cornmeal Muffins

MAKES 14

8 slices bacon

4 tablespoons butter

4 tablespoons margarine

1 cup flour

1 tablespoon baking powder

1 teaspoon sugar

¼ teaspoon salt

1½ cups cornmeal

1 cup milk

2 eggs

1 Preheat the oven to 400°F. Grease 14 muffin cups or use paper liners.

2 ▲ Fry the bacon until crisp. Drain on paper towels, then chop into small pieces. Set aside.

3 Gently melt the butter and margarine and set aside.

4 ▲ Sift the flour, baking powder, sugar, and salt into a large mixing bowl. Stir in the cornmeal, then make a well in the center.

5 In a saucepan, heat the milk to lukewarm. In a small bowl, lightly whisk the eggs, then add to the milk. Stir in the melted fats.

6 ▼ Pour the milk mixture into the center of the well and stir until smooth and well blended.

7 ▲ Fold in the bacon.

8 Spoon the batter into the prepared cups, filling them halfway. Bake until risen and lightly colored, about 20 minutes. Serve hot or warm.

Rosemary Bread

MAKES 1 LOAF

1 × ¼ oz package dried fast-action yeast

1½ cups whole-wheat flour

1½ cups self-rising flour

2 tablespoons butter, plus more to grease bowl and pan

¼ cup warm water (110°F)

1 cup milk, whole or 2% (room temperature)

1 tablespoon sugar

1 teaspoon salt

1 tablespoon sesame seeds

1 tablespoon dried chopped onion

1 tablespoon fresh rosemary leaves, plus more to decorate

1 cup cubed Cheddar cheese

coarse salt, to decorate

1 ▼ Mix the fast-action yeast with the flours in a large mixing bowl. Melt the butter. Stir in the warm water, milk, sugar, butter, salt, sesame seeds, onion, and rosemary. Knead thoroughly until quite smooth.

2 ▲ Flatten the dough, then add the cheese cubes. Quickly knead them in until they have been well combined.

3 Place the dough into a clean bowl greased with a little butter, turning it so that it becomes greased on all sides. Cover with a clean, dry cloth. Put the greased bowl and dough in a warm place for about 1½ hours, or until the dough has risen and doubled in size.

4 Grease a 9- × 5-inch loaf pan with the remaining butter. Knock down the dough to remove some of the air, and shape it into a loaf. Put the loaf into the pan, cover with the clean cloth used earlier and leave for about 1 hour until doubled in size once again. Preheat the oven to 375°F.

5 Bake for 30 minutes. During the last 5–10 minutes of baking, cover the loaf with foil to prevent it from becoming too dark. Remove from the loaf pan and leave to cool on a wire rack. Decorate with rosemary leaves and coarse salt scattered on top.

~ **VARIATION** ~

For Tarragon bread, substitute 1 tablespoon chopped fresh tarragon for the rosemary, and 1 cup goat cheese for the Cheddar cheese.

Orange Wheat Loaf

MAKES ONE 1 LB LOAF

| 2¼ cups whole-wheat flour |
| 1/2 teaspoon salt |
| 2 tablespoons butter |
| 2 tablespoons light brown sugar |
| 1/2 package dried fast-action yeast |
| grated rind and juice of 1/2 orange |

1 ▲ Sift the flour into a large bowl and return any wheat flakes from the sifter. Add the salt and rub in the butter lightly with your fingertips.

2 ▲ Stir in the sugar, yeast, and orange rind. Pour the orange juice into a measuring jug and make up to 7/8 cup with hot water (the liquid should not be more than hand hot).

3 ▼ Stir the liquid into the flour and mix to a soft ball of dough. Knead gently on a lightly floured surface.

4 Place the dough in a greased 1 lb loaf pan and leave in a warm place until nearly doubled in size. Preheat the oven to 425°F.

5 Bake the bread for 30–35 minutes, or until it sounds hollow when you tap the loaf underneath. Tip out of the pan and cool on a wire rack.

~ **FREEZER NOTE** ~

To freeze, wrap tightly in foil when still warm, then leave to cool completely before freezing. Keeps for up to one year.

Corn Bread

1 cup flour

⅓ cup sugar

1 teaspoon salt

1 tablespoon baking powder

1½ cups cornmeal

1½ cups milk

2 eggs

6 tablespoons butter, melted

8 tablespoons margarine, melted

1 Preheat the oven to 400°F. Line the bottom and sides of a 9- × 5-inch loaf pan with wax paper and grease.

2 Sift the flour, sugar, salt, and baking powder into a mixing bowl.

3 ▼ Add the cornmeal and stir to blend. Make a well in the center.

4 ▲ Whisk together the milk, eggs, butter, and margarine. Pour the mixture into the well. Stir until just blended; do not overmix.

5 Pour into the pan and bake until a cake tester inserted in the center comes out clean, about 45 minutes. Serve hot or at room temperature.

Tex-Mex Corn Bread

3–4 whole canned chili peppers, drained

2 eggs

2 cups buttermilk

4 tablespoons butter, melted

½ cup flour

1 teaspoon baking soda

2 teaspoons salt

1½ cups cornmeal

2 cups corn kernels

1 Preheat the oven to 400°F. Line the bottom and sides of a 9-inch square cake pan with wax paper and grease lightly.

2 ▲ With a sharp knife, chop the chilies in a fine dice and set aside.

3 ▲ In a large bowl, whisk the eggs until frothy, then whisk in the buttermilk. Add the melted butter.

4 In another large bowl, sift together the flour, baking soda, and salt. Fold into the buttermilk mixture in 3 batches, then fold in the cornmeal in 3 batches.

5 ▲ Fold in the chilies and corn.

6 Pour the batter into the prepared pan and bake until a cake tester inserted in the middle comes out clean, 25–30 minutes. Let stand for 2–3 minutes before unmolding. Cut into squares and serve warm.

Brown Soda Bread

MAKES ONE 2 LB LOAF

4 cups flour
3 cups whole-wheat flour
2 teaspoons salt
1 tablespoon baking soda
4 teaspoons cream of tartar
2 teaspoons sugar
4 tablespoons butter
up to 3¾ cups buttermilk or skim milk
extra whole-wheat flour, to sprinkle

1 Lightly grease a baking sheet. Preheat the oven to 375°F.

2 ▼ Sift the flour, salt, baking soda, cream of tartar and sugar into a large bowl, tipping any bran from the flour back into the bowl.

3 ▲ Rub the butter into the flour mixture, then add enough buttermilk or milk to make a soft dough. You may not need all of it, so add it cautiously.

4 ▲ Knead lightly on a floured surface until smooth then transfer to the baking sheet and shape to a large round about 2-inch thick.

5 ▲ Using the floured handle of a wooden spoon, form a large cross on top of the dough. Sprinkle over a little extra whole-wheat flour.

6 Bake for 40–50 minutes until risen and firm. Cool for 5 minutes before transferring to a wire rack to cool further.

Sage Soda Bread

MAKES 1 LOAF

2 cups whole-wheat flour
1 cup flour
½ teaspoon salt
1 teaspoon baking soda
2 tablespoons shredded fresh sage or 2 teaspoons dried sage, crumbled
1¼–1¾ cups buttermilk

1 ▲ Preheat the oven to 425°F. Sift the flour, salt and baking soda into a large bowl.

2 ▲ Stir in the sage and add enough buttermilk to make a soft dough.

~ **COOK'S TIP** ~

As an alternative to the sage, try using finely chopped fresh rosemary or thyme.

3 ▼ Shape the dough into a round loaf and place on a lightly oiled cookie sheet.

4 ▲ Cut a deep cross in the top. Bake in the oven for 40 minutes until the loaf is well risen and sounds hollow when tapped on the bottom. Leave to cool on a wire rack.

Zucchini Crown Bread

SERVES 8

1 lb zucchini, coarsely grated

salt

5 cups flour

2 packages dried fast-action yeast

4 tablespoons Parmesan cheese, freshly grated

ground black pepper

2 tablespoons olive oil

lukewarm water, to mix

milk, to glaze

sesame seeds, to garnish

1 Spread out the zucchini in a colander and sprinkle lightly with salt. Leave to drain for 30 minutes, then pat dry.

2 Meanwhile, grease and line a 9-in round cake pan, and then preheat the oven to 400°F. Mix the flour, yeast and Parmesan together and season with black pepper.

3 ▲ Stir in the oil and zucchini and add enough lukewarm water to give you a good firm dough. Knead the dough on a lightly floured surface until it is smooth.

4 ▲ Leave it to rise in a warm place until doubled in size. Break into eight balls, rolling each one and placing them in the tin as shown. Brush the tops with milk and sprinkle over the sesame seeds.

5 Allow to rise again, then bake for 25 minutes or until golden brown. Cool slightly in the pan, then turn out the bread to cool further.

Rosemary Focaccia

SERVES 4

1 lb package white bread mix

4 tablespoons extra virgin olive oil

2 teaspoons dried rosemary, crushed

8 sun-dried tomatoes, snipped

12 black olives, pitted and chopped

¾ cup lukewarm water

sea salt flakes

~ **VARIATION** ~

For Gremolata Focaccia, substitute 2 tablespoons chopped fresh parsley for the dried rosemary, 2 tablespoons capers for the sun-dried tomatoes, and add 1 crushed garlic clove to the dough.

1 ▲ Mix the bread mix with half the oil, the rosemary, tomatoes, olives and water until it forms a firm dough.

2 Turn out the dough onto a lightly floured surface and knead thoroughly for 5 minutes. Return the dough to the mixing bowl and cover.

3 Leave the dough to rise in a warm place until it has doubled in size. Meanwhile, lightly grease two baking sheets with olive oil and preheat the oven to 425°F.

4 ▼ Turn out the risen dough, punch down and knead again. Divide into two and shape into rounds. Place on the baking sheet, and punch hollows in the dough. Trickle over the remaining olive oil and sprinkle with salt.

5 Bake the focaccia for 12–15 minutes until golden brown and cooked. Slide off onto wire racks to cool. Eat slightly warm.

Focaccia with Onions

SERVES 6–8

3 cups flour

1 package dried fast-action yeast

1 teaspoon salt

pinch of sugar

5 tablespoons olive oil

1 medium onion, sliced very thinly and cut into short lengths

½ teaspoon fresh thyme leaves

coarse sea salt

1 Place the flour, yeast, salt and sugar in a bowl. Make a well in the center and pour in 1 cup of lukewarm water and 1 tablespoon of the oil. Mix to a dough and knead on a floured surface until smooth and elastic.

2 Place the dough in a large oiled bowl, cover with plastic wrap and leave in a warm place until doubled in size. Knead the dough on a floured surface for 3–4 minutes.

3 ▼ After punching the dough down, knead it for 3–4 minutes. Brush a large shallow baking pan with about 1 tablespoon of the oil. Place the dough in the pan, and use your fingers to press it into an even layer 1-inch thick. Cover the dough with a clean cloth, and leave to rise in a warm place for about 30 minutes. Preheat the oven to 400°F during this time.

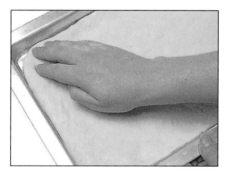

4 ▲ While the focaccia is rising, heat 3 tablespoons of the oil in a medium frying pan. Add the onion, and cook over low heat until soft. Stir in the thyme.

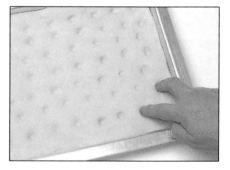

5 ▲ Just before baking, use your fingers to press rows of indentations into the surface of the focaccia. Lightly brush the focaccia all over with the remaining oil.

6 ▲ Spread the onions evenly over the top, and sprinkle lightly with coarse salt. Bake for about 25 minutes, or until just golden. Cut into squares or wedges and serve as an accompaniment to a meal, or alone, warm or at room temperature.

Zucchini and Parmesan Bread

MAKES 1 LOAF

1¼ cups flour
1 cup whole-wheat flour
2 teaspoons baking powder
1 teaspoon salt
1 teaspoon ground cumin
1 teaspoon fennel seeds
8 oz (2 medium) zucchini, grated
⅔ cup vegetable oil
2 eggs, beaten
3 tablespoons milk
⅔ cup grated Parmesan cheese
1 teaspoon sesame seeds
salt and black pepper

1 ▲ Preheat the oven to 350°F. Grease a 2-lb loaf pan and line the base. Sift the flour, whole-wheat flour, baking powder, salt, and ground cumin into a bowl and tip in any bran left in the sifter.

3 ▼ Whisk together the oil, eggs, milk and half the cheese in a bowl. Stir into the zucchini mixture.

2 ▲ Add the fennel seeds, followed by the grated zucchini.

4 ▲ Spoon the mixture into the prepared pan and level the top. Sprinkle the top with the remaining Parmesan cheese. Bake for 40–45 minutes, until risen and when a skewer pierced through the center comes out clean. Serve hot or cold.

Italian Bread Sticks

MAKES ABOUT 30

1 tablespoon fresh cake yeast or
⅓ package active dried yeast

½ cup lukewarm water

pinch of sugar

2 teaspoons malt extract (optional)

1 teaspoon salt

1¾–2 cups white unbleached flour

1 ▲ Warm a medium mixing bowl by swirling some hot water in it. Drain. Place the yeast in the bowl, and pour on the warm water. Stir in the sugar, mix with a fork, and allow to stand until the yeast has dissolved and starts to foam, 5–10 minutes.

2 ▲ Use a wooden spoon to mix in the malt extract, if using, the salt and about one-third of the flour. Mix in another third of the flour, stirring with the spoon until the dough forms a mass and begins to pull away from the sides of the bowl.

3 ▲ Sprinkle some of the remaining flour onto a smooth work surface. Remove all of the dough from the bowl, and begin to knead it, working in the remaining flour a little at a time. Knead for 8–10 minutes. By the end the dough should be elastic and smooth. Form it into a ball.

4 ▲ Tear a lump the size of a large walnut from the ball of dough. Roll it lightly between your hands into a small sausage shape. Set it aside on a lightly floured surface. Repeat until all the dough is used up. There should be about 30 pieces.

~ **VARIATION** ~

Bread sticks are also good when rolled lightly in poppy or sesame seeds before being baked.

5 ▲ Place one piece of dough on a clean smooth work surface without any flour on it. Roll the dough under the spread-out fingers of both hands, moving your hands backward and forward to lengthen and thin the dough into a long strand about ⅜ inch thick. Transfer to a very lightly greased cookie sheet. Repeat with the remaining dough pieces, taking care to roll all the bread sticks to about the same thickness.

6 ▲ Preheat the oven to 400°F. Cover the tray with a cloth, and place the bread sticks in a warm place to rise for 10–15 minutes while the oven is heating. Bake for about 8–10 minutes. Remove from the oven. Turn the sticks over, and return them to the oven for 6–7 minutes more. Do not let them brown. Allow to cool. Bread sticks should be crisp when served. If they lose their crispness on a damp day, warm them in a moderate oven for a few minutes before serving.

Saffron Focaccia

MAKES 1 LOAF

pinch of saffron threads
2/3 cup boiling water
2 cups flour
1/2 teaspoon salt
1 teaspoon dried fast-action yeast
1 tablespoon olive oil
FOR THE TOPPING
2 garlic cloves, sliced
1 red onion, cut into thin wedges
rosemary sprigs
12 black olives, pitted and coarsely chopped
1 tablespoon olive oil

1 ▲ Place the saffron in a heatproof cup and pour on the boiling water. Leave to stand and infuse until lukewarm.

~ VARIATION ~

For Herb Focaccia, substitute 2 tablespoons chopped fresh mixed herbs, such as parsley, thyme, chives, and basil, for the rosemary. Use 2 tablespoons sun-dried tomato paste instead of the olives.

2 ▲ Place the flour, salt, yeast and olive oil in a food processor. Turn on and gradually add the saffron and its liquid. Process until the dough forms into a ball.

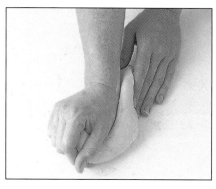

3 ▲ Turn onto a floured board and knead for 10–15 minutes. Place in a bowl, cover and leave to rise for 30–40 minutes until doubled in size.

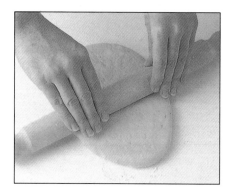

4 ▲ Punch down the risen dough on a lightly floured surface and roll out into an oval shape, 1/2-inch thick. Place on a lightly greased cookie sheet and leave to rise for 20–30 minutes.

5 ▲ Preheat the oven to 400°F. Just before baking, press small indentations all over the surface of the focaccia with your fingers.

6 ▲ Cover with the topping ingredients, brush lightly with olive oil, and bake for 25 minutes or until the loaf sounds hollow when tapped on the bottom. Leave to cool on a wire rack.

~ COOK'S TIP ~

Dried fast-action yeast usually contains an improver such as vitamin C, and the dough will probably need only one rising. Some brands, however, may require two risings, so check the package before you begin.

Focaccia with Olives

SERVES 6–8

FOR THE BASIC DOUGH

3 cups flour

1 package dried fast-action yeast

1 teaspoon salt

pinch of sugar

3 tablespoons olive oil

FOR THE TOPPING

10–12 large green olives, pitted and
    halved lengthwise

coarse sea salt

1 Place the flour, yeast, salt and sugar in a bowl. Make a well in the center and pour in 1 cup of lukewarm water and 1 tablespoon of the oil. Mix to a dough and knead on a floured surface until smooth and elastic.

2 Place dough in a large oiled bowl, cover with plastic wrap and leave in a warm place until doubled in size. Turn out the dough on to a floured surface and knead for 3–4 minutes.

3 Brush a large shallow baking pan with 1 tablespoon of the oil. Place the dough in the pan, and use your fingers to press it into an even layer 1-inch thick.

4 ▲ Cover the dough with a cloth, and leave to rise in a warm place for 30 minutes. Preheat the oven to 400°F during this time. Just before baking, use your fingers to press several rows of light indentations into the surface of the focaccia. Brush with the remaining oil.

5 ▲ Dot evenly with the olive pieces, and sprinkle with a little coarse salt. Bake for about 25 minutes, or until just golden. Cut into squares or wedges and serve as an accompaniment to a meal, or alone, warm or at room temperature.

~ COOK'S TIP ~

For a delicious sandwich, split the focaccia in half, horizontally, and fill with sliced mozzarella cheese, sliced tomatoes, and fresh basil leaves.

Focaccia with Rosemary

SERVES 6–8

1 quantity Basic Dough, risen once (see
    above)

3 tablespoons olive oil

2 sprigs fresh rosemary, coarse stalks
    removed

coarse sea salt

1 After punching the dough down, knead it for 3–4 minutes. Brush a large shallow baking pan with 1 tbsp of the oil. Place the dough in the pan, and use your fingers to press it into an even layer 1 inch thick.

2 ▲ Scatter with the rosemary leaves. Cover the dough with a cloth, and leave to rise in a warm place for 30 minutes. Preheat the oven to 400°F during this time.

3 ▼ Just before baking, use your fingers to press rows of light indentations into the surface of the focaccia. Brush with the remaining oil, and sprinkle lightly with coarse salt. Bake for about 25 minutes, or until just golden. Cut into squares or wedges and serve as an accompaniment to a meal.

Italian Olive Bread

MAKES 1 LOAF

3 cups flour

½ teaspoon salt

1 teaspoon dried fast-action yeast

1 teaspoon dried thyme

3 tablespoons olive oil

4 black or green olives, pitted and chopped

3 sun-dried tomatoes in oil, drained and chopped

crushed rock salt

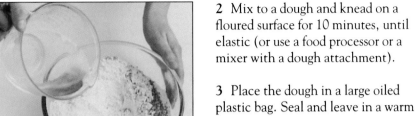

1 ▲ Place the flour and salt in a bowl and sprinkle over the yeast and thyme. Make a well in the center and then pour in ⅞ cup warm water and 2 tablespoons of the olive oil.

2 Mix to a dough and knead on a floured surface for 10 minutes, until elastic (or use a food processor or a mixer with a dough attachment).

3 Place the dough in a large oiled plastic bag. Seal and leave in a warm place for about 2 hours, or until the dough has doubled in size.

4 ▲ Turn out the dough on a floured surface and knead lightly. Flatten the dough with your hands. Sprinkle over the olives and tomatoes and knead them in until they are well distributed. Shape the dough into a long oval and place on a lightly greased baking sheet. Cover and leave to rise in a warm place for 45 minutes. Preheat the oven to 375°F.

5 ▲ When risen, press your finger several times into the dough, drizzle over the remaining oil and sprinkle with the salt. Bake for 35–40 minutes, until the loaf is golden and sounds hollow when tapped on the bottom.

Tomato Bread Sticks

MAKES 16

2 cups flour

½ teaspoon salt

½ tablespoon dried fast-action yeast

1 teaspoon honey

1 teaspoon olive oil

⅔ cup warm water

6 pieces sun-dried tomatoes in olive oil, drained and chopped

1 tablespoon skim milk

2 teaspoons poppy seeds

1 Place the flour, salt and yeast in a food processor. Add the honey and olive oil and, with the machine running, gradually pour in the water (you may not need it all as flours vary). Stop adding water as soon as the dough starts to cling together. Process for 1 minute more.

2 ▲ Turn out the dough onto a floured board and knead for 3–4 minutes until springy and smooth.

3 ▲ Knead in the chopped sun-dried tomatoes. Form into a ball and place in a lightly oiled bowl. Leave to rise for 5 minutes.

4 ▼ Preheat the oven to 300°F. Divide the dough into 16 equal pieces and with your fingers, roll each piece into an 11- × ½-inch long stick. Carefully transfer to a lightly oiled cookie sheet and leave to rise in a warm place for 15 minutes.

5 ▲ Brush the sticks with milk and sprinkle with poppy seeds. Bake for 30 minutes. Leave to cool on a wire rack.

BISCUITS
& POPOVERS

At their best when warm from the oven, biscuits
needn't be confined to simple buttermilk or
traditional varieties. Cheese biscuits, enlivened by
the addition of fresh or dried herbs, or Sunflower
Sultana Biscuits are some of the imaginative recipes
included here. As a change from individual Yorkshire
puddings, try tangy Parmesan Popovers for a cheesy
treat. Eat with a roast or simply as a tasty snack.

Buttermilk Biscuits

MAKES 15

1½ cups flour

1 teaspoon salt

1 teaspoon baking powder

½ teaspoon baking soda

4 tablespoons cold butter or margarine

¾ cup buttermilk

1 Preheat the oven to 425°F. Grease a baking sheet.

2 Sift the dry ingredients into a bowl. Cut in the butter or margarine with a pastry blender until the mixture resembles coarse crumbs.

3 ▼ Gradually pour in the buttermilk, stirring with a fork to form a soft dough.

4 ▲ Roll out about ½ inch thick.

5 Stamp out 2-inch circles with a cookie cutter.

6 Place on the prepared tray and bake until golden, 12–15 minutes. Serve warm or at room temperature.

Baking Powder Biscuits

MAKES 8

1⅓ cups flour

2 tablespoons sugar

3 teaspoons baking powder

⅛ teaspoon salt

5 tablespoons cold butter, cut in pieces

½ cup milk

1 Preheat the oven to 425°F. Grease a baking sheet.

2 ▲ Sift the flour, sugar, baking powder, and salt into a bowl.

3 Cut in the butter with a pastry blender until the mixture resembles coarse crumbs.

4 Pour in the milk and stir with a fork to form a soft dough.

~ **VARIATION** ~

For Berry Shortcake, split the biscuits in half while still warm. Butter one half, top with lightly sugared fresh berries, such as strawberries, raspberries or blueberries, and sandwich with the other half. Serve with dollops of whipped cream.

5 ▲ Roll out the dough about ¼ inch thick. Stamp out circles with a 2½-inch cookie cutter.

6 Place on the prepared sheet and bake until golden, about 12 minutes. Serve hot or warm, with butter for meals; to accompany tea or coffee, serve with butter and jam.

Cheese and Marjoram Biscuits

MAKES 18

1 cup whole-wheat flour

1 cup self-rising flour

pinch of salt

scant 3 tablespoons butter

¼ teaspoon dry mustard

2 teaspoons dried marjoram

½–⅔ cup finely grated sharp Cheddar cheese

½ cup milk, or as required to make soft dough

1 teaspoon sunflower oil (optional)

⅓ cup pecans or walnuts, chopped

1 ▼ Gently sift the two kinds of flour into a bowl and add the salt. Cut the butter into small pieces, and rub these into the flour until it resembles fine bread crumbs.

2 ▲ Add the mustard, marjoram and grated cheese, and mix in sufficient milk to make a soft dough. Knead the dough lightly.

3 Preheat the oven to 425°F. Roll out the dough on a floured surface to about a ¾-inch thickness and cut it out with a 2-inch square cutter. Grease some cookie sheets with the paper from the butter (or use a little sunflower oil), and place the biscuits on the sheets.

4 Brush the biscuits with a little milk and sprinkle the chopped pecans or walnuts over the top. Bake for 12 minutes. Serve warm.

~ **VARIATION** ~

For Mixed Herb and Mustard Biscuits, with a light, summery flavor, use 2 tablespoons chopped fresh parsley or chives in place of the dried marjoram. Use 1 teaspoon Dijon mustard and ⅓ cup chopped pistachios for the dry mustard and the pecans.

Cheese and Chive Biscuits

MAKES 9

1 cup self-rising flour
1 cup self-rising whole-wheat flour
½ teaspoon salt
3 oz feta cheese
1 tablespoon snipped fresh chives
⅔ cup skim milk, plus extra for glazing
¼ teaspoon cayenne pepper

1 ▲ Preheat the oven to 400°F. Sift the flours and salt into a mixing bowl, adding any bran left over from the flour in the sifter.

2 ▲ Crumble the feta cheese and rub into the dry ingredients. Stir in the chives, then add the milk and mix to a soft dough.

3 ▼ Turn out the dough onto a floured surface and lightly knead until smooth. Roll out to ¾-inch thick and stamp out nine scones with a 2½-inch cookie cutter.

4 ▲ Transfer the biscuits to a nonstick baking sheet. Brush with skim milk, then sprinkle over the cayenne pepper. Bake in the oven for 15 minutes, or until golden brown. Serve warm or cold.

Whole-Wheat Biscuits

MAKES 16

¾ cup (1½ sticks) cold butter

2 cups whole-wheat flour

1 cup all-purpose flour

2 tablespoons sugar

½ teaspoon salt

2½ teaspoons baking soda

2 eggs

¾ cup buttermilk

¼ cup raisins

1 Preheat the oven to 400°F. Grease and flour a large baking sheet.

2 ▲ Cut the butter into small pieces.

3 Combine the dry ingredients in a bowl. Add the butter and cut in with a pastry blender until the mixture resembles coarse crumbs. Set aside.

4 In another bowl, whisk together the eggs and buttermilk. Set aside 2 tablespoons for glazing.

5 Stir the remaining egg mixture into the dry ingredients until it just holds together. Stir in the raisins.

6 Roll out the dough about ¾ inch thick. Stamp out circles with a cookie cutter. Place on the prepared sheet and brush with the glaze.

7 Bake until golden, 12–15 minutes. Allow to cool slightly before serving. Split in two with a fork while still warm and spread with butter and jam, if wished.

Orange Raisin Biscuits

MAKES 16

2 cups flour

1½ tablespoons baking powder

⅓ cup sugar

½ teaspoon salt

5 tablespoons butter, diced

5 tablespoons margarine, diced

grated rind of 1 large orange

⅓ cup raisins

½ cup buttermilk

milk, for glazing

1 Preheat the oven to 425°F. Grease and flour a large baking sheet.

2 Combine the dry ingredients in a large bowl. Add the butter and margarine and cut in with a pastry blender until the mixture resembles coarse crumbs.

3 ▲ Add the orange rind and raisins.

4 Gradually stir in the buttermilk to form a soft dough.

5 ▲ Roll out the dough about ¾ inch thick. Stamp out circles with a cookie cutter.

6 ▲ Place on the prepared sheet and brush the tops with milk.

7 Bake until golden, 12–15 minutes. Serve hot or warm, with butter or whipped cream, and jam.

> **~ COOK'S TIP ~**
>
> For light tender scones, handle the dough as little as possible. If you wish, split the scones when cool and toast them under a preheated broiler. Butter them while still hot.

Sunflower-Raisin Biscuits

MAKES 10–12

2 cups self-rising flour

1 teaspoon baking powder

2 tablespoons soft sunflower margarine

2 tablespoons sugar

⅓ cup raisins

2 tablespoons sunflower seeds

⅔ cup plain yogurt

about 2–3 tablespoons skim milk

1 Preheat the oven to 450°F. Lightly oil a cookie sheet. Sift the flour and baking powder into a bowl and rub in the margarine evenly.

2 Stir in the sugar, raisins, and half the sunflower seeds, then mix in the yogurt, with just enough milk to make a fairly soft, but not sticky dough.

3 ▼ Roll out on a lightly floured surface to about ¾-inch thickness. Cut into 2½-inch flower shapes or rounds with a cookie cutter and lift onto the baking sheet.

4 ▲ Brush with milk and sprinkle with the reserved sunflower seeds, then bake for 10–12 minutes, until puffed and golden brown.

5 Cool the biscuits on a wire rack. Serve split and spread with butter and jam.

Prune and Candied Peel Cookies

MAKES 12

2 cups flour

2 teaspoons baking powder

⅔ cup raw sugar

½ cup chopped dried prunes

⅓ cup chopped candied citrus peel

finely grated rind of 1 lemon

¼ cup sunflower oil

5 tablespoons skim milk

~ **VARIATION** ~

For Spicy Fruit Cookies, substitute ½ cup dried cranberries for the prunes, ⅓ cup raisins for the candied peel, and add 1 teaspoon apple pie spice, ¼ teaspoon ground ginger, and ¼ teaspoon ground cinnamon.

1 ▼ Preheat the oven to 400°F. Lightly oil a large baking sheet. Sift together the flour and baking powder, then stir in the sugar, prunes, peel, and lemon rind.

2 Mix the oil and milk, then stir into the mixture, to make a dough which just binds together.

3 ▲ Spoon rough mounds onto the baking sheet and bake for 20 minutes, until golden. Cool on a wire rack.

Dill-Potato Cakes

MAKES 10

2 cups self-rising flour

3 tablespoons butter, softened

pinch of salt

1 tablespoon finely chopped fresh dill

scant 1 cup mashed potato, freshly made

2–3 tablespoons milk, as required

1 ▼ Preheat the oven to 450°F. Sift the flour into a bowl, and add the butter, salt and dill. Mix in the mashed potato and enough milk to make a soft, pliable dough.

2 ▲ Roll out the dough on a well-floured surface until it is fairly thin. Cut into several neat rounds with a 3-inch cutter.

3 ▲ Grease a cookie sheet, place the cakes on it, and bake for 20–25 minutes until risen and golden.

> ~ **VARIATION** ~
>
> For Cheese and Herb Potato Cakes, blue cheese makes a tasty addition. Stir in about ¼ cup crumbled blue cheese, and substitute 1 tablespoon snipped fresh chives for the dill. In place of the butter, use 3 tablespoons sour cream.

Parmesan Popovers

MAKES 6

½ cup freshly grated Parmesan cheese
1 cup flour
¼ teaspoon salt
2 eggs
1 cup milk
1 tablespoon butter or margarine, melted

1 ▼ Preheat the oven to 450°F. Grease six ¾-cup popover pans. Sprinkle each pan with 1 tablespoon of the grated Parmesan. Alternatively, you can use custard cups, in which case, heat them on a baking sheet in the oven, then grease and sprinkle with Parmesan just before filling.

2 Sift the flour and salt into a small bowl. Set aside.

3 ▲ In a mixing bowl, beat together the eggs, milk, and butter or margarine. Add the flour mixture and stir until smoothly blended.

4 ▼ Divide the batter evenly among the pans, filling each one about half full. Bake for 15 minutes, then sprinkle the tops of the popovers with the remaining grated Parmesan cheese. Reduce the heat to 350°F and continue baking until the popovers are firm and golden brown, 20–25 minutes.

5 ▲ Remove the popovers from the oven. To unmold, run a thin knife around the inside of each pan to loosen the popovers. Gently ease out, then transfer to a wire rack to cool.

Herb Popovers

MAKES 12

3 eggs

1 cup milk

2 tablespoons butter, melted

¾ cup flour

⅛ teaspoon salt

1 small sprig each mixed fresh herbs, such as chives, tarragon, dill, and parsley

1 Preheat the oven to 425°F. Grease 12 small ramekins or popover cups.

2 With an electric mixer, beat the eggs until blended. Beat in the milk and melted butter.

3 Sift together the flour and salt, then beat into the egg mixture to combine thoroughly.

4 ▼ Strip the herb leaves from the stems and chop finely. Mix together and measure out 2 tablespoons. Stir the herbs into the batter.

5 ▲ Fill the prepared cups half-full.

6 Bake until golden, 25–30 minutes. Do not open the oven door during baking time or the popovers may fall. For drier popovers, pierce each one with a knife after the 30 minute baking time and bake for 5 minutes more. Serve hot.

Cheese Popovers

MAKES 12

3 eggs

1 cup milk

2 tablespoons butter, melted

¾ cup flour

¼ teaspoon salt

¼ teaspoon paprika

6 tablespoons freshly grated Parmesan cheese

~ **VARIATION** ~

To make Yorkshire Pudding Popovers, as an accompaniment for roast beef, omit the cheese, and use 4–6 tablespoons of the pan drippings to replace the butter. Put them into the oven in time to serve warm with the beef.

1 Preheat the oven to 425°F. Grease 12 small ramekins or popover cups.

2 ▲ With an electric mixer, beat the eggs until blended. Beat in the milk and melted butter.

3 ▲ Sift together the flour, salt, and paprika, then beat into the egg mixture. Add the cheese and stir.

4 Fill the prepared cups half-full and bake until golden, 25–30 minutes. Do not open the oven door during baking or the popovers may fall. For drier popovers, pierce each one with a knife after the 30 minute baking time and bake for 5 minutes more. Serve hot.

INDEX

~